Asheng
Archive

1

Jane Good

S.B. Publications

Fifty per cent of royalties to be donated to the
Ashenground Community Centre.

*I would like to dedicate this book to
my grandmother Beatrice Swaby.*

First published in 2008 by S. B. Publications
Tel: 01323 893498
Email: sbpublications@tiscali.co.uk
www.sbpublications.co.uk

2

ISBN 978-185770-3382

Designed and Typeset by EH Graphics (01273) 515527

Front cover photos: *Ashenground Meadows, Great Poplar field, Bridle path,
Bluebells and Orchid.*

Title page photo: *Keeper's Cottage, Ashenground Road.*

Back cover photo: *Steam train approaching Ashenground Bridge, 2007.*

The lush green meadows, the meandering streams
Soon Ashenground fields will exist only in dreams.
The grazing rabbits, the graceful, leaping deer
Whose habitats very soon will all disappear.
A summer stroll in the meadows is as good as it gets
Hopefully this book will remind you when the sun finally sets.

3

Ashenground Badgers

Acknowledgments

I would like to thank the following people for helping me compile this book:-
The owner of Great Haywards Farmhouse for allowing me to photograph his property.
Carol Martin for the photos of Bolnore.
Eileen Keast for the photos of Ashenground Meadows in the snow.
Marianne Griffin for help with the history of the convent.
Stuart Meier for the deer in the snow photo and help with the history of the area.
Mary Hopper for help with my rusty English grammar.
My husband Ian for taking the photos and and helping me with the computer side of this project.
The staff of Haywards Heath library for showing me their old maps of the area.
The nuns of the Convent of The Holy Cross for lending me a book on their history.
And finally I would like to thank everyone who has shared their memories with me and put up with my endless questions because without them there would be no book.

Great Haywards Farm

Contents

Following the recent public enquiry (ending May 2007) 'Four Acre Meadow' has reverted back to its original name of 'Four Acre Wood'. This is due to its increasing woodland cover.

The stream running through the centre of Ashenground Woods known as 'Furnace Brook' has recently also been called 'Foundry Brook'.

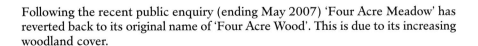

Ashenground Archive - A Pictorial History

Introduction

At a first glance the area now known as Ashenground may appear quite ordinary, even uninteresting. There is an area of woodland and a few fields separated by a primitive track which is usually unbelievably muddy. But then first appearances can very often be deceptive. A large part of the woodland is ancient, consisting of many native trees including beech and mature oak. The track was once an important bridleway known as the King's Highway. On the 1638 Manorial Map of Haywards Heath the route of it is described as leading to Cuckfield, Lewes and Brighthelmstone. It is edged with very old hornbeam trees. The five associated meadows are a rare and valuable habitat as unimproved and water meadows are fast disappearing from the Sussex countryside. These meadows are home to many mammals, insects and flowers. There are badgers and rabbits, in the woods, deer and dormice and a great variety of birds.

As if all the above wasn't important enough it seems that in the 1500s the meadow areas were, if not part of the original Heath (or Hoth as it used to be called), at least very similar in appearance to it. The earliest reference to the town was in the 1200s when the surname Hayworth was first recorded. Hayworth meant an enclosure for keeping animals which were used for sport.

These meadows were land belonging to Great Haywards farmhouse which, along with Little Haywards farmhouse, were built around 1400 and owned by Nicholas Hardham in the seventeenth century - both these properties still exist today. Great Haywards farmhouse is at the top of Great Haywards Field and is just visible from what remains of Duncton Meadow while Little Haywards has now become part of Courtlands, a road off Haywards Road. Haywards Road used to be called Little Haywards Road after the farmhouse.

The course of an important Roman road, the London-Brighton Way, wends its way through Bolnore and passes to the west of Beech Hurst and Lucastes. The road was used by the military and also for the transportation of iron ore and agricultural produce. A few years ago the course of the road indicated by an agger (i.e. a Roman embankment) was clearly visible. While there are many really good books about the history of Haywards Heath there seems to be very little documented about the area of Ashenground itself. Therefore the area I am covering in this book extends from Great Haywards in the north, the London to Brighton railway line in the east, Ashenground Woods and Bolnore Village in the south and Bolnore Road in the west.

I moved to the Ashenground area of Haywards Heath from London in the spring of 1984. I had lived in a West London suburb not far from Heathrow and had chosen this area to live for two reasons. The first being it was a commutable distance for my husband to travel to London and the second was I knew and liked the area as my grandparents had retired to nearby Hurstpierpoint many years earlier. It really was my dream to live in such a rural market town after living under the flight path to Heathrow. The first I learned about the existence of Ashenground Woods was from the owner of the house in Sheppeys that we have owned since our move.

During the last twenty-two years I have walked around Ashenground Wood and meadows on most days and noticed many changes. Unlike walking in a park one is never sure about what one may encounter. Every season and each different time of day brings different sights. If we are lucky we may stumble across a few deer or a fox. I have seen snakes hiding under logs, weasels, mice and too many rabbits to mention. I have pictures of resident badgers and there must be at least a dozen species of birds. Often we see or hear woodpeckers and occasionally a flock of goldfinches. Owls can be heard sometimes and in the autumn swallows can be seen swooping over the meadows. I suppose rabbits are the animals most likely to be seen in the meadows - I can't help but think of "Watership Down" when I see them running.

A Brief History

Ashenground Wood is not really Ashenground Wood at all, it is an amalgamation of Catt's Wood and Pierce's Wood. The real Ashenground Wood was where Ashenground housing estate is now. Ashenground Wood is recognised as a site of Nature Conservation. The name Ashenground is believed to come from the ash on the ground resulting from the brick workings in the area. On the 1874 map of Haywards Heath a brickfield, pug mill and a kiln are shown on the area which now lies east of the junction of Haywards Road and Ashenground Road. The ground would have been covered in ash from the firing of the bricks in the kilns. The tithe map of 1845 shows the woodland areas to the east and west of the railway line as being owned by William Catt and the land being of twenty-six and twenty-seven acres respectively. The strip of land to the west of the railway line was owned by the railway company. On this tithe map Sheppeys farmhouse and garden was owned by Stephen Bine and occupied by Thomas Betts. This same farmhouse was previously owned by James Cooke who died in 1813. It was sold in 1824 along with his many other holdings in the local area including the Heaselands estate. It was described as being in the parish of Keymer and called Sherries or Sheppeys but formerly called Iswoods or Fielders. It had a messuage (i.e. a dwelling house), garden, barn and other buildings and had 26 acres of arable, meadow and woodland and was occupied by a Richard Pierce at a yearly rent of £24-3s. The estate was entitled to "Rights of Commonage upon the extensive wastes of the Manor of Keymer". The heath became enclosed in 1861. Sheppeys farmhouse later became known as Rumbell's Cottage as shown on the 1874 map but it reverted back to the name of Sheppeys before being demolished around 1957.

At the beginning of the nineteenth century Haywards Heath was just a wasteland with a few farmhouses but that all changed with the building of the railway between 1837 and 1841. The first government census of 1841, in which the town is split between the parishes of Cuckfield, Wivelsfield and Keymer, shows that a large percentage of the population were railway workers(see figs. 1 and 2). Many were casual workers, some born locally but many were drafted in from other places. From the 1841 census it can be seen that many lived in "cottages on the railroad". Many cottages were built in the 1860s for the workers in the local brick industry. In 1894 Victorian villas were being built for wealthy commuters travelling to London and Brighton.

The meadows still have the appearance that they would have had in medieval times with their ancient field patterns. The acreage of the meadows to be included in the local plan for building is about sixty acres. In the early 1800s the local estate map shows Great Haywards Heath Farm as 163 acres and Little Haywards Heath Farm as 24 acres. The names of the meadows are given as Four Acre Wood (now Four Acre Meadow), The Lag (now North Meadow), Four Acres and Maze Field (Great Haywards Field), Lower Readings Field and Crabtree Field (Chapel Field) and Lower Eight Acres and Little Wood (Great Poplar Field).

The woods have changed a great deal over the last twenty years - nature never stands still. The hurricane of 1987 evoked many changes as one in every five trees in Sussex came down that October evening. Where mighty oaks fell, large glades opened up woodland floor to the light encouraging new plants to prosper. The progression of flowers is always the same - the dwarf yellow daffodils, the white wood anemones and then the bluebells. I am sure our bluebell woods are amongst the finest in England, especially on a lovely spring morning when the air is filled with their scent - I think it is the closest thing to heaven you can wish for. The woodland paths change direction constantly as people and animals vary their tracks. The meadows are slowly reverting to woodland with the absence of grazing animals. When I first walked the meadows there were cattle grazing and people recall horses grazing in the past. One of the reasons for my wanting to compile this book is that at the time of writing outline planning permission had been granted for 785 homes to be built on the area immediately surrounding Ashenground Wood. The whole area is set to change from a rural to a residential one. Chapel Field, Great Poplar Field and Great Haywards Field are to be built on. Building on Four Acre Meadow is subject to a public enquiry and North Meadow is to have balancing ponds to prevent flooding. Land to the south west of the woods has already been extensively built on being occupied with Bolnore Village. It used to be forestry commission land and was covered in pine trees and purple foxgloves and had far-reaching views to the South Downs. This land was owned by the Kleinwort family before being sold to Crest Nicholson and the public was discouraged from walking on it. The public were given Ashenground Wood for their recreation (there was a plaque hanging on a tree in the woods dedicating it to them).

The ancient bridle path which separates the woods from the meadows is about to be resurfaced and lighting is to be installed. It will be crossed by roads in two places between Bolnore Village and Farm to allow lorries access into the meadows for the development. One road has been marked out with polythene fences and there are traps for great-crested newts. There will be no more wading through the mud on wet mornings - but isn't that what country living is all about?

If I cannot help prevent the development of Ashenground and the loss of the countryside maybe the least I can do is provide a photographic record for the current and future residents of Haywards Heath who perhaps will share the same interest in the past as I have. Finally, I would like to end with a quote from the local wildlife photographer Stephen Dalton. I showed him around Ashenground Wood and meadows in 1994 and he said "those who live in the town are fortunate to have such an accessible place of spiritual renewal on their doorstep". I think this quote is just perfect.

Jane Good

2007

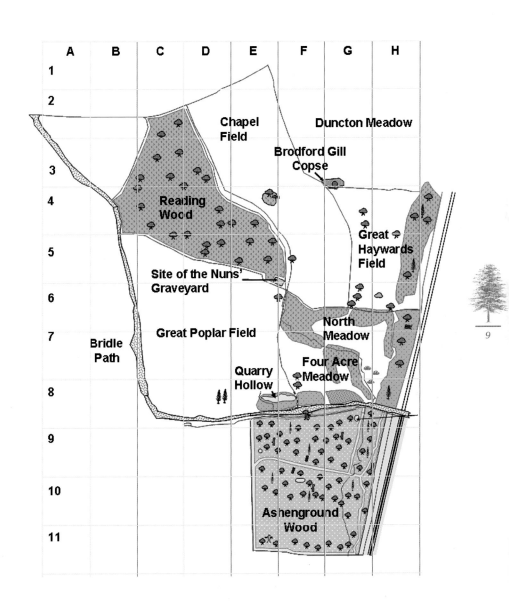

	A	B	C	D	E	F	G	H

1

2

Chapel
Field

Duncton Meadow

Brodford Gill
Copse

3

4

Reading
Wood

Great
Haywards
Field

5

Site of the Nuns'
Graveyard

6

Great Poplar Field

North
Meadow

7

Bridle
Path

Four Acre
Meadow

Quarry
Hollow

8

9

10

Ashenground
Wood

11

9

Haywards Heath Occupations 1841 (Census) - By Category

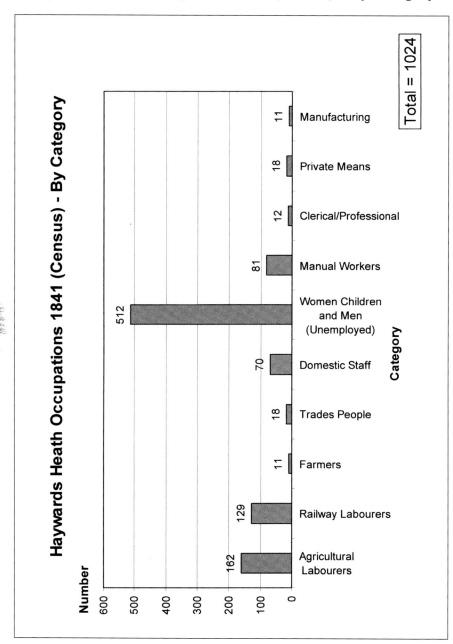

Total = 1024

Haywards Heath Occupations 1841 (Census) - By Category

Category	Number
Manufacturing	11
Private Means	18
Clerical/Professional	12
Manual Workers	81
Women Children and Men (Unemployed)	512
Domestic Staff	70
Trades People	18
Farmers	11
Railway Labourers	129
Agricultural Labourers	162

Figure 1.

Haywards Heath Occupations - 1841 (Census)

Occupation	Number
Children (under 18)	319
Women (no occupation recorded)	175
Agricultural Labourers	162
Railway Labourers	109
Female Servants	39
Labourers	32
Male Servants	21
Miners	20
Independents	18
Men (no occupation recorded)	18
Brickmakers	16
Carpenters	11
Farmers	11
Bricklayers	9
Grocers	7
Masons	7
Shoemakers	5
Millers	4
Police Constables	4
Blacksmiths	3
Gardeners	3
Housekeepers/ Cooks	3
Butchers	2
Clerks	2
Drapers	2
Engineers	2
Footmen and Grooms	2
Tinkers	2
Bailiffs	1
Beer Shop Keepers	1
Bookmakers	1
Builders	1
Butlers	1
Contractors	1
Inn Keepers	1
Inspectors	1
Lawyers	1
Maltsters	1
Nurses	1
Printers	1
Store Keepers	1
Tea Dealers	1
Timber Merchants	1
Toll Collectors	1
Total	**1024**

Figure 2.

Sunrise over Ashenground

Sunrise over Reading Wood. Chapel Heights is just visible far right. [F4]

Early morning in Great Poplar Field. [D8]

The Early Years

My sons Richard and Paul climbing an old tree on the edge of Four Acre Meadow shortly after our arrival here in 1984.

[F7]

A clearing in the centre of Ashenground Wood.   [F9]

This stream is known as Furnace Brook and is brown in colour due to the iron in the soil. The stream is a tributary of the River Adur and it flows through the centre of one of the oldest parts of Ashenground Wood.   [G8}

An early view of Four Acre Meadow looking towards North Meadow. Note the fence dividing the meadow which has now disappeared to be replaced by bushes and small trees.   [G7]

Views of Ashenground woods and meadows

Path into Four Acre Meadow, formerly Four Acre Wood, as indicated on the 1874 Ordnance Survey map of the area. [G8]

South West corner of Four Acre Meadow looking towards Quarry Hollow with the BMX track beside it. An ecologist found that when surveyed in 2006 this meadow had at least nineteen ancient woodland indicators e.g. bluebells and wood anemones. [F7]

North Meadow looking back towards Four Acre Meadow. The unimproved acid grassland found here is a very rare habitat in Sussex, especially when it is associated with ancient woodland. [G6]

The fallen log dividing North Meadow from Great Haywards Field. The hedgerow on the right appears very old - some have been dated to the 1200s. [G6]

Scots pine trees on the railway embankment in Great Haywards Field.
[H5]

The deep well which is hidden in woodland (Brodford Gill Copse) between Chapel Field and Great Haywards Field. It probably belonged to the now-demolished Victorian-built Oakwood House.
[G3]

View from the top of Chapel Field showing panoramic views to the South Downs. Before the hedge on the left was planted there was a metal fence of which remnants can still be seen. [G4]

North Meadow shown here is gradually reverting to woodland. This meadow has been grazed on and off for the last forty or fifty years but in the life of an ancient woodland this is a relatively short time. [G6]

Blue Belle leads the way immediately left from the railway bridge adjacent to the railway line. [H8]

This part of the woods is ancient (i.e. woodland that has existed since or before 1600). Note the railway and houses of Sheppeys in the background. Sheppeys takes its name from a farmhouse that used to stand on what is now Vale Road allotments. [G8]

A view of the bridle path beyond Ashenground Bridge looking towards Bolnore Village. Four Acre Meadow is on the right and the stream on the left.   [G8]

The white wood anemones carpet the woodland floor along with the purple fritillary far right.   [G8]

Along the path next to the stream which runs alongside Ashenground Wood. After heavy rain this stream flows really fast. [G8]

The last remaining daffodils of spring in a glade close to the perimeter fence next to Bolnore Village. [E9]

This mound in Ashenground Wood is probably the remains of a building platform of an ancient house. According to the 1638 manorial map of Haywards Heath a Thomas Davis had a house here.   [E9]

A photo of Butcher's Broom, an ancient woodland plant which is growing in what would have been the garden of the house of Thomas Davis. It is so called because its mature branches used to be tied in a bundle and used to sweep floors.   [E9]

A fallen tree in the centre of Ashenground Wood which was probably brought down by the hurricane of 1987.   [E8]

A view from the bridle path looking towards Ashenground railway bridge.   [G8]

The fallen tree in the stream in the centre of Ashenground Wood. This tree has been in the same position since the hurricane.   [G9]

Celandine in the woods. Its companion plants of bluebells, Saint John's Wort and wood anemones are all ancient woodland indicators.   [G8]

The wicket fence on the left of the woodland path was made by the "The Friends of Ashenground and Bolnore Woods" in 2006.   [G10]

The stream flood plain in the centre of Ashenground Wood. This area probably hasn't changed much in the last few hundred years.   [G10]

The bridle path with trees leaning at various angles. Great Poplar Field is on the right and Bolnore Village on the left. [D8]

The pond to the left of the bridle path adjacent to Bolnore Village. Various forms of wildlife are often seen here including dragonflies. [D8]

The ancient bridle path towards Bolnore Farm and Village. This section of the bridle path used to be known as "Half Street Lane" in 1638 apparently because the owners of the two farms either side had to share it. [C8]

View across Great Poplar Field towards Reading Wood and Chapel Field. Beyond the western edge of this field are a few cottages which were built around 1900 for some of the workers at the convent. One of these cottages is called St Stephens reflecting the name of the convent's orphanage. [C8]

Wending my way up the bridle path trying not to disappear in the mud. The bridle path becomes quite sunken beyond this point. [C8]

There used to be a sheep enclosure at the top left corner of Great Poplar Field. Beyond this stood the convent's water tower as it did not have running water until 1970. [C7]

The top of Great Poplar Field with the rooftops of Bolnore Village just visible. A map of 1910 shows the nuns of the Holy Cross Convent had market gardens extending from Reading Wood down across the top of this field covering around a third of it. [C8]

A view into Reading Wood where it is believed some deer may live. In the spring of 1911 a biplane carrying Gordon England, who lived at Oakwood, crashed into Reading Wood. [D4]

The nuns' graveyard looking towards Great Poplar Field. The Mother Foundress of the Holy Cross Convent was buried here in 1957, her body being transferred from St Wilfrid's graveyard. [F5]

Reading Wood from Chapel Field showing the stream in the foreground which the nuns remember flooding. This wood used to be known as both Reading Coppice and Rushy Grove and it used to join up with Four Acre Wood at this point. [F6]

View of Chapel Field with Bolnore Road and then Beech Hurst in the distance. A retired nurses' home is just visible in the distance. Purple rhododendrons appear in the hedgerow in spring. [F5]

Chapel Field was named after the conventual church or chapel which used to belong to the Holy Cross Convent. The convent was built between 1887 and 1902 and it housed St Stephen's Orphanage which had its origins in Wapping, East London. Around 1980 due to falling numbers the nuns moved to Leicester and the buildings are now privately owned and called Chapel Heights and Grosvenor Hall. [F4]

The top of Great Haywards Field looking towards Duncton Meadow, of which half has been taken for modern housing. Although not the original Great Haywards Farm's orchard, walkers remember pear and apple trees on this site in Duncton Meadow.   [G4]

Large oak tree in Great Haywards Field. A stream known as Brodford Gill runs along the top of this field to the right of this photo.   [G4]

The hedgerows covered in may blossom along the edge of Great Haywards Field.
[G6]

Fallen branch across the path at the southern edge of Great Haywards Field. To the left of the picture the remains of an old metal gate were found as well as an old metal boundary fence still in situ. [G6]

A view of the hedgerows in Great Haywards Field looking towards Bolnore Village. [G4]

Gorse bush in Great Haywards Field. Mr Arthur Pannett, an authority on local history, in 1937 described Haywards Heath as "a wasteland of gorse and heather which was interspersed with Scotch firs and had a windmill at the highest point." [H5]

Our grandson Ben next to the fallen tree on the railway embankment. This fallen tree is known to us as Molly, Tess and Dusty's seat as their owner Carole used to take a rest there. [H6]

The steep hill leading to the second part of the railway embankment. This steep incline was created by the spoil from the railway cutting. [H6]

View along the railway embankment towards Wealden Way. [H5]

Winter

The snow fell silently this morning
It doesn't usually come over our way
So be sure to get out and enjoy it
For very shortly it all will have melted away.

Snow on the bridle path near Ashenground Bridge.

Both of these photos were taken in March 1995. This one is of Great Haywards Field.

[G6]

The large black poplar tree from which Great Poplar Field takes its name.

[D8]

The bridle path next to Ashenground bridge collapsed into the stream below one winter as it had rained so much. [H8]

View through the centre of the woods after the hurricane of 1987. [F9]

A family walk along the bridle path past the ancient hornbeams alongside Four Acre Meadow. [G8]

Spring

Are they purple or are they blue?
The bluebells that fill every glade.
Only one thing is certain they will soon be gone
When the woodland in summer returns to shade.

Bluebells in Ashenground Wood

Spring

These bluebells in Ashenground Wood are what spring is all about. Their colour and scent are impossible to capture in a photograph.   [F9]

This lone primrose appears every year in spring beside the path through the centre of the woods.   [F9]

The woodland path is beginning to turn green again. [F9]

43

A mixture of wood anemones, bluebells and white bluebells. [G8]

Bluebells as far as the eye can see in the centre of the woods. [E10]

A glade edged with bluebells in the centre of the woods. [G10]

Summer

Meandering through the wild flower meadow
Pausing for breath under the shade of the old oak trees
Lost in a world of so long ago
Memories are made of times just like these

Great Haywards Field in summer.

The purple hue of the meadow grass in Great Poplar Field. [E7]

Buttercups and other wild flowers in Great Haywards Field. [G4]

One of the purple orchids in Great Haywards Field.

[H6]

A rarer white orchid. The orchids are mainly found in Four Acre Meadow, North Meadow and Great Haywards Field. In 2006 some were found in Great Poplar Field.

[H6]

View from the wooden bridge on the bridle path looking towards Four Acre Meadow. [G8]

Autumn

The magic spell of autumn has been cast
Of cobwebs and of mist and fungi
The leaves have descended upon us
Another year has almost passed by.

Autumn magic in Ashenground Wood.

Autumn

From one acorn to mighty oaks. Oaks predominate in Ashenground because of their liking for clay soil.   [H8]

The trees in Ashenground Wood just beginning to turn for autumn.   [E9]

View along the bridle path showing clearly the new course and the original course on the left next to the hornbeam trees. [F8]

The autumn leaves begin to carpet the bridle path. [G8]

An early view of the bridle path near Ashenground bridge before the undergrowth was cleared to make it wider.

[H8]

A frosty morning at the junction of Great Poplar Field and Chapel Field. One of the former nuns at the Convent of the Holy Cross remembers "beating the bounds" around these fields when she lived here.   [F5]

Blue Belle in the autumn leaves in Ashenground Wood.   [F8]

One of the many grey squirrels in the area. This wildlife photo should have been of a nuthatch but this squirrel chased it off to steal the show. This tree is the tall Scots pine by the new thatched cottage in Bolnore Village next to the bridle path. [C8]

An early photo of the entrance to Four Acre Meadow. [G8]

Another early photo of Four Acre Meadow before all the trees began to reappear. [F8]

Blue Belle and Bella on a frosty morning in Great Poplar Field. [E6]

Looking towards the old oak tree in Great Poplar Field. [D8]

Nature's Bounty

Blackberries are always abundant in the meadows in late summer with plenty for everyone.   [G6]

Rosehips in the hedgerows of Great Haywards Field.   [G6]

The colourful sight of the guelder-rose in Great Haywards Field.　　　　[H5]

An apple tree in Four Acre Meadow which perhaps appeared from the seeds discarded by the horses that used to graze here.

[G8]

Elderberries and holly at the junction of North Meadow, Great Haywards Field and Chapel Field. [G6]

Fungi in the morning dew in Chapel Field. [F4]

Large holly tree in Great Haywards Field not far from the old well.　　　[G4]

Relics of the past

An old gate post on the bridle path by the thatched cottage on the edge of Bolnore Village. [B7]

An original gate and post found lying abandoned in a ditch between Great Haywards Field and North Meadow. [G6]

The remains of an old bridge in the stream between Four Acre Meadow and North Meadow. [F7]

An old track way running between Chapel Field and North Meadow. [G6]

Illuminated tree stump by the rope swing near to the centre of Ashenground Wood.
[F8]

Atmospheric Ashenground

The sun shining through the trees alongside the railway embankment in Great Haywards Field. [H4]

A perfect spider's web in the meadows. [G7]

Bracket fungus on an old tree in the centre of Ashenground Wood.   [E10]

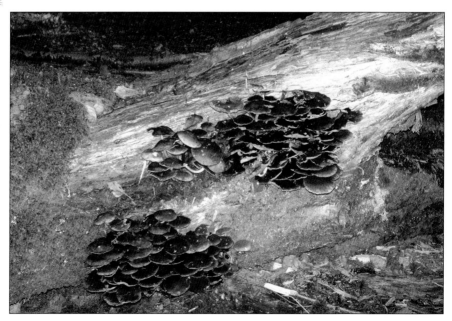

Fungi on a fallen tree in Ashenground Wood.   [E10]

One of the many spooky faces to be found on the hornbeam trees edging the bridle path. [F8]

Large fungus growing out of a tree stump in Ashenground Wood. [F8]

Path through the centre of Ashenground Wood heading for Bolnore Village.[G9]

The beginning of the end. The sun sets over the workings to construct a road crossing the bridle path which will bring in the heavy goods vehicles to start the next phase of house building.   [C8]

Tree spirit near the middle of Ashenground Wood.
[F9]

Autumn colours in Four Acre Meadow. [G8]

The tall chimney of Great Haywards Farmhouse is just visible on the left beyond Duncton Meadow. This farmhouse has dominated the history of this area for almost six hundred years.   [G3]

The London to Brighton Railway looking towards Rocky Lane Bridge and ultimately Brighton. The railway dissected Great Haywards and Little Haywards Farms when it was built between 1837 and 1841.   [H8]

These buildings which originally belonged to the Convent of the Holy Cross stand on Bolnore Road adjacent to Chapel Field at the top of Reading Wood.   [C2]

These nuns' gravestones have been moved and can be found at the side of the cemetery at the southern tip of Reading Wood. Most have the inscription Mary on them.   [F5]

A roe deer in the snow in Catt's Wood which lies to the west of Ashenground Wood.

The duck pond at the bottom of the garden of Great Haywards Farmhouse. A stream running into this pond wends its way down to Great Haywards Field.[G3]

Changes

An early picture of North Meadow showing the absence of trees. An ancient track way runs along the top left of this field where it borders Chapel Field.   [G7]

Many years later small trees are establishing themselves in North Meadow. [G7]

Lush green grass and trees in Great Poplar Field.   [E6]

The drought takes its toll on Great Poplar Field robbing it of its colour.   [E6]

Places of special interest

The enormous oak tree in Great Poplar Field. [E6]

One of the orchids that regularly
appear in the uncut meadow grass.
[H6]

Quarry Hollow is a deep pit that is usually full of murky water. It was on the map as long ago as 1638 and was probably dug for clay for the local brick and tile-making industries and also for sandstone for building. It could also have been dug for marl which was used on the land as a fertilizer. [E8]

This dead tree on the railway embankment attracts the woodpeckers.

[H5]

Ferns line the path on the way to the stream where the southern tip of Ashenground Wood joins Pierce's Wood. There are many dried-up stream beds on the southern edge of Ashenground Wood. [F11]

Oakwood Road, which was the original track from Muster Green leading to Great Haywards Farmhouse. [G2]

Me standing outside Great Haywards Farmhouse which was built around 1450. It has changed very little over the centuries although much of its original grounds are lost to modern housing. A few old pear trees remain in the garden, perhaps the remnants of the orchards and market gardens that once surrounded the house.

[G3]

Ashenground Activities

Children have made a BMX track next to Quarry Hollow giving the area the appearance of a lunar landscape.   [F8]

Making snowmen in Four Acre Meadow.   [G7]

Cross country runners and joggers are often spotted - sometimes with dogs in pursuit.   [H8]

A rope swing has been made at the edge of Ashenground Wood so the children can swing over the stream.   [F8]

There is always plenty of wildlife to see - an example is this red admiral butterfly on the bluebells. [E7]

One can go train spotting from the embankment walks. Bella's tail points to the direction of the trains. [G10]

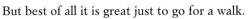

But best of all it is great just to go for a walk.   [D8]

Bolnore

Holly off for a walk in the snow over Bolnore.

These fields used to be Forestry Commission land and were covered in Scots pine trees.

Bolnore looking towards the South Downs - a view that has virtually disappeared now since the housing took place.

I remember seeing all the purple foxgloves when I used to walk over this land.

The sun sets on Ashenground

View of the sun beginning to set on the meadows. The old oak tree to the right of centre in this photo is about three hundred and fifty years old. [E6]

The sun finally sets over Ashenground Meadows, casting a shadow over the black poplar tree that has been towering over this field for about a hundred and fifty years - but no one knows for how much longer. [D8]

Memories

The nuns graveyard pre 1957

The Nuns' Graveyard pre-1957

There are a few aerial photos showing the Ashenground area as it was in the 1930s and 1940s. The obvious difference from today's landscape is how wooded the area was then, particularly around Four Acre Meadow which joined up to Reading Wood. The nuns' allotments ran down in strip formation covering the top third of Great Poplar Field. The nuns apparently farmed Great Poplar Field and Chapel Field up to about 1948 when the land was leased to the Heaseland estate. The photos show a fence running along the boundary of Great Haywards Field and Chapel Field. This fence has since been replaced with a hedge. There also appears to be a large formal garden to the front of what was Oakwood House which now has retirement flats on it. The dense wooded areas of Great Haywards and Little Haywards Woods are very prominent in the foreground of the photos and many of the significant oaks still standing today can be identified.

I have asked some of the more senior local residents to recall their memories of Ashenground to me. This chapter of the book covers an area to include the Ashenground housing estate. I have omitted the residents' names to protect their identity but I am extremely grateful to them for sharing their recollections with me. Most begin by saying they have few valuable memories of the Ashenground area that I am covering but they then go on to tell me anecdotes that may to them seen unimportant but collectively they form a bigger picture of what life was really like. One Sheppeys resident tells me of happy days in the early sixties when she and her young daughters would spend whole days picnicking in Ashenground Wood. They would go with their friends or neighbours and take sandwiches and jellies with

Children from Sheppeys on a day out in Ashenground Wood in the early 1960s. Sandy Harris is in the centre of the picture.

Children sitting on one of the seats in Ashenground Wood including Sandy's sister Carol in the centre foreground.

them. They would paddle in the stream and sit on the seats that were built in the wood. On other occasions the children would ride their bikes into the water in the dip that is now known as Quarry Hollow but used to be known as the "Poolsy". Apparently it was called the Poolsy after the landowner Mr Poole, who would ride around on horseback. There was also a very deep hollow filled with beech leaves adjacent to the path running through the centre of Ashenground Wood which the children used to run up and down in the early sixties. She recalls there were Bee Orchids on the land running between the embankments and the footpath turning immediately left just over the railway bridge, and she also tells me the steam engines passing would regularly set the embankments alight causing the firemen to run down her garden to extinguish the flames. The grass on these embankments would be cut every so often to try to prevent these fires. She recalls how vast the Kleinwort estate used to be as in the early part of the century there were a couple of estate workers' cottages in Rocky Lane and then just open fields up to the Keeper's cottage on Ashenground Road. My neighbour tells me how highly respected Lady Kleinwort was as she would always help any deserving cause.

One elderly lady whose late husband spent his life working on the Heaseland estate has shared some of her memories with me. She lived in the "Old House" on Rocky Lane. The house was divided into two cottages, an old widow lived in one and she and her husband in the other, and it was very isolated. Her first recollection is of listening to the nightingales at night. Once when walking down Wivelsfield Road, passing the top of Ashenground Road, an old man said to her "I remember this place when it was all cornfields". She remembers the boy scouts singing in the evenings by the camp fire in what is now Rumbolds Lane and then in the early morning the clattering sound as they were getting breakfast. She remembers her husband harvesting and ploughing in the fields which are now the roads Holmbush, Kilnbarn and Burchetts. She says that these roads were named after farms on the Heaseland Estate, where her husband worked on the land for forty-three years.

This estate used to stretch as far as Burgess Hill and Cuckfield. This lady remembers taking her children for long walks in the woods where Bolnore Village is now - they would pick chestnuts which they would roast on the fire. They were always on the lookout for deer which they were told were there but they never saw (she thinks they were probably too noisy to see them). She said nobody ever bothered them. She remembers the long summer of 1963 there. She recalls having snow that lasted a long time and all the children from Sheppeys as well as her own would go sledging in the steepest field close to Old House. There were one or two accidents including one to one of her friends who still today has the scar from a cut lip.

Another neighbour living in Ashenground Road tells me she remembers when she first moved into the area in 1955 she saw the woodcutter walk by every morning. He would leave his house, the keeper's cottage, on the corner of Ash Grove, carrying his black kettle slung over his shoulder ready for his day's work in the woods. She tells me how in her youth she worked as a court dressmaker in Ashenground House. She also recalls a house called Keymer End which was almost next to Ashenground House in Ashenground Road but she didn't go down to Ashenground Wood in those days as it was just a muddy track leading to it. Prefabs were built in the woods in the 1950s where Sunnywood Drive now is and the road Wood Ride was so named because it was a ride or track way through the wood. Some of the original trees still exist in the gardens of Wood Ride.

A postcard of the entrance to the Holy Cross Convent sent in 1905. The chapel on the left had just been completed in 1902.

A similar view taken in 2007

Another former resident tells me that when he was a child in the fifties he knew the Ashenground Wood of today as big Ashenground Wood and the area where the Ashenground estate now is as little Ashenground Wood. He recalls a scout hut being on the site of where Ash Grove now is. Another local person tells me there used to be a tinker's cottage where Sheppeys was built. A few people tell me they remember playing by the stream in the woods where the Church of the Ascension now stands on the corner of Vale Road and Sheppeys. The original residents of Sheppeys when asked for their memories repeatedly recall nostalgic picnics in Ashenground Wood and often refer to the nice seats they used to have there. One couple remember how Ashenground Wood was fenced off when the Kleinwort's gave it to the people of Haywards Heath (probably in the 1950s) and how a plaque was put up informing them that the wood was given to them. They remember how the Heaseland land that Bolnore Village stands on was planted with many trees including Christmas trees. They remember seeing tame badgers on this land and tell of hearing the horn on the land announcing the arrival of the local hunt. They remember seeing the residents of the elderly peoples' homes at Oakwood putting food out for the badgers, who would eat it and then the local foxes would finish up anything that was left. Sheppeys residents recall there being a nursery next to Beech Hurst where plants would be grown for local parks. One lady in Sheppeys tells me she remembers snowdrops growing in the nuns' graveyard in Reading Wood and beautiful azaleas in the gardens that used to surround the convent. The masses of bluebells and wild daffodils featured in people's memories and of how Rocky Lane could be reached directly from Ashenground Wood.

One eighty-five-year-old former resident of Ashenground recalls how the nuns would frequently visit Muster Green in their pony and trap selling their own produce of fruit, vegetables and honey. She remembers this from around seventy or eighty years ago. I have since been told that this pony was called Lady Jane.

A lady from Park Road has heard stories of how herds of cattle were led from Bolnore Farm along Bolnore Road then down Paddockhall Road to the market opposite Haywards Heath Station where the supermarket now stands. I have been told that others remember the cattle being driven from the market up Boltro Road, along South Road and Sussex Road ending up at the slaughter house on the corner of Triangle Road where a funeral parlour is now situated.

One Sheppeys couple have been telling me about the land where the Ashenground estate is now. They remember the time when the Vale Road allotments used to be nurseries and how there was a stream running down what is now Vale Road and Rumbolds Lane. This stream (which has now been culverted) had beech trees along its embankments and it flowed under the railway line into Furnace Brook in the present day Ashenground Wood. The couple remember having picnics by this stream and remember the woods leading to the railway being of thicket and hazel which was regularly coppiced. This area of woodland they knew as Sheppeys Wood while the wood they called Ashenground was around where Wood Ride and Sunnywood Drive now stand. They remember being allowed to play in the farmer's fields opposite Rumbolds Lane where Acre Close stands. They were cornfields and had the sheaves of corn standing up to dry - in the winter the children would toboggan down these fields. There were memories of noisy steam goods trains thundering past their house late in the evening - with so many carriages the trains seemed endless. The couple recall many ponies being kept in Ashenground meadows - some would be ridden in the meadows while others would be taken

A photo taken *c*.1950 of the farmer who lived in the "Old House" on Rocky Lane. He had worked for the Heaseland Estate, where the photo was taken, for forty-three years and was a champion ploughman of Sussex.

This peaceful scene of cattle grazing on land adjoining "Old House" in Rocky Lane. It was taken about twenty-five years ago in the 1980s.

elsewhere to be ridden and people on horseback were a familiar sight down Sheppeys. After the ponies had left the fields the cattle arrived but these cows were for beef not for milk. They remember the bluebells in the wood.

One former resident tells me how he remembers the old house Beech Hurst being demolished in the 1950s and of how the existing walled car park used to contain potting sheds. The Beech Hurst miniature railway shed now stands on what was the stable block. One local resident in her nineties tells me of the horse mushrooms that used to grow in large numbers in Ashenground meadows during the time the ponies grazed there. This lady who lives in one of the Art Deco houses in Sunnywood Drive tells me they were the first houses to be built there and were built in the 1930s in Great Haywards Wood and were reached by what was then just an unmade track. These houses were built as holiday homes for Londoners and at least one house still has a servant's buzzer in the living room. There were just half a dozen houses built and the houses on the east side of the road still contain many trees from the original wood in their back gardens. She remembers a large white building known as Drummond House standing on the top of the hill where Drummond Close now stands. This house was surrounded by a few smaller properties, one she remembers was called Bundoo. She tells me she remembers hearing the nightingales singing around the large house. She remembers the prefabs, which were built in Sunnywood Drive after the Second World War, being demolished in 1963 and how the local children would rush onto Ashenground Bridge to watch the frequent sight of the fireman putting out the railway embankment fires. She tells me of the wild strawberries growing in vast numbers on the land where Bolnore Village has been built. She also recalls seeing the remains of a stone structure about thirty feet by fifteen feet on the land beyond the fence where Bolnore Village is - she wonders if it was the remains of an old house or a garden pond, but it has now completely disappeared.

She tells of how people were told off for trespassing if they ventured onto the land where Bolnore Village is. Children would hide behind the bushes if they heard the sound of the owner's horses approaching. This lady found an old horse shoe on the path by the railway line leading up to Rocky lane and she still has this in her possession. She remembers many redwood trees being on the Kleinwort land up to the 1980s but then they just disappeared and also remembers seeing pear trees in Chapel Field(the 1896 map of Haywards Heath shows a small orchard on this field). She tells me there used to be wild garlic under the giant oak tree in Great Poplar Field. She too thinks that there has been a decline of some species of birds especially fieldfares and bullfinches but she still remains impressed by the variety of shrubs and trees in Ashenground, in particular sweet chestnut and horse chestnut trees, the many crab apple trees, wild cherry trees and the blackthorns. She tells me she remembers a long time ago seeing many pheasants from the Kleinwort Estate settling down for the night in Ashenground Wood.

I received a letter from one gentleman who grew up in the Ashenground area and whose great-grandfather and great-grandmother started to work for the sisters of Holy Cross Convent when it began as a home for destitute girls in the East End of London. The gentleman's great-grandparents then came to Haywards Heath in 1887 when the convent was built. His grandfather, father and elder brother all worked for the Sisters at the Holy Cross Convent and his niece and her husband still work for the Sisters today at their new home in Leicestershire. He moved to live in St Stephens cottage by the convent in 1932. The Ashenground Wood that

A view of cows grazing beyond Sandy Vale in the 1980s.

The construction of Bolding Way between Sandy Vale and Rocky Lane in the 1980s. Twenty-five years later this area is now covered with houses and Bolnore Village houses dominate the distant views.

he was familiar with just consisted of the track and trees that joined Ashenground Road with Isaacs Lane. He continues to say that the woods that are called Ashenground Wood were Pierce's Wood and Catt's Wood and were part of the Bolnore Estate. They could not gain access to these woods as they were fenced off and Mr Pickett the gamekeeper was often on hand to keep them out. He says the only people who seemed to gain access were the gypsies who picked all the wild daffodils and sold them in bunches in South Road.

They played in the old Ashenground Wood as children and also in the pits adjoining the Convent fields in what they called Poole's Wood - these pits originally had quite a lot of water in and he can remember ducks and moorhens nesting in the banks (these pits are now known as Quarry Hollow and Poole's Wood was where Four Acre Wood used to be and was so called because the owner of Great Haywards Farm had the surname Poole). This gentleman is the only person I have spoken to who remembers the trees actually being felled in what is now Four Acre Meadow. He believes these pits were quarries from which rocks were taken for building purposes and he has also told me the story of another pit that was situated at the side of Ashenground Wood near the Convent Farm. This pit is shown on old maps and the convent used it to dump all their rubbish - originally it was quite deep. Apparently this gentleman's brother dumped his old Austin 10 car there in about 1960 so the archaeologists will have quite a find when they do their survey before the house building. He says that it was not possible to get all the Sisters out of the cemetery at Reading Wood so the convent still own the land and have let it revert to nature. I am told there was a second keeper's cottage belonging to a Mr Tollhurst which was situated along the bridle path towards Isaacs Lane on the left just before Bolnore Farm. This cottage still stands today. This gentleman tells me that on the convent site there was a well tower situated where there are now offices - this well was a least a hundred and twenty feet deep and was from where the convent and the surrounding cottages had their water pumped. There was an underground stream running under there which kept a steady supply of water for the convent's needs. To supply the convent's electricity there was also an engine shed which supplied power for the pumps for the water and power for the generator for the electricity. He remembers one day walking down Bolnore Road and being confronted by a herd of cows that had escaped and he had to lead them all into a the field where Beech Hurst golf course is now and close the gate on them.

One lady in her eighties who has lived in Sheppeys for over fifty years recalls how the variety of wildlife has diminished. She remembers when nightingales sang in Ashenground Wood just beyond the railway bridge when she first lived here in the 1950s. She remembers seeing grey partridges and pheasants in the woods and meadows, but she feels there are less foxes, hedgehogs and slowworms now as she rarely sees them in her garden. She recalls early morning visits to the meadows to pick the mushrooms.

The present owner of Great Haywards Farmhouse has told me of how many years ago the farmhouse had fallen into disrepair and the then owners had vacated it and built a new residence to live in. An 1896 map of Haywards Heath shows a large house and a lodge (the 1948 aerial photo of the area shows a large driveway and extensive formal gardens). The house was named Great Haywards and was situated just northeast of the original farmhouse near to Muster Green. On the 1901 census there is a Great Haywards House listed as being in Great Haywards

A view of the Convent before the Chapel was built in 1902.

The pony and trap from which the Sisters sold produce from their gardens and farm.

Road (probably what is now called Oakwood Road). The owners of the house were two sisters in their sixties who were born in Essex. Their staff are listed as a lady's maid, parlour-maid, cook, housemaid and a scullery maid . Their ages range from fourteen to forty-two. The domestic staff at Great Haywards Farmhouse are listed as gardeners, groom, cowman, waiter, housekeeper and a coachman. There is no trace of Great Haywards House or the Lodge now - a modern housing estate has been built on the land.

A large house named Oakwood is listed next to Great Haywards Farmhouse. There are quite a few large properties listed in Bolnore Road in 1901 including Belvedere School, Glencoe, Beechfield, Hazelmere, Ferndale and St Helena. St Helena's Retreat was a guest house for the Holy Cross Convent and is now a nursing home named Ashton House. The entry for the convent describes it as The Holy Cross Home which is for the training of young servants. The census which was recorded on 31st March 1901 stated there were about thirty sisters of mercy, a matron, a certified school mistress, a sick nurse and five servants. There were fifty-three inmates who came from all over the country and they were aged between six and eighteen. The houses named Beechfield, Ferndale and Hazelmere still exist and have the same names today. I am told that in the past the nuns let the boys from Belvedere School play football in Chapel Field after lessons had finished. Beyond Ashton House the farm workers' cottages still stand.

One lady who was born in 1942 and now lives in Sandy Vale has been telling me her memories. She grew up in Haywards Heath and remembers when there were two main businesses in Ashenground Road - one was the court dressmakers in Ashenground House and the other was a company called Spirella which made corsets from a house near the top of the road. She recalls having heard that during the Second World War children from Great Ormond Street Hospital were evacuated to a large house called Elfinsward which was situated on the corner of Bolnore Road where the police station is now. This lady remembers what lovely old houses Beech Hurst and Clevelands were and she remembers the beehives at Little Haywards Farm where children were given honeycombs to take home. She remembers all the wells in the area and of how her father, who had a plumbing apprenticeship for the local builder Thomas White, would earn half-a-crown a week and get an extra sixpence a week for lining a well with bricks.

Nightingale   *Bee Orchid*   *Horse Mushroom*

Haymaking on the Convent Farm featuring two generations of the Nichols family. The building behind was part of the cowsheds and has now been converted to a cottage.

Oakwood House - a view across Duncton Meadow *c.*1904.